COLOR OUR HAIRSTYLES

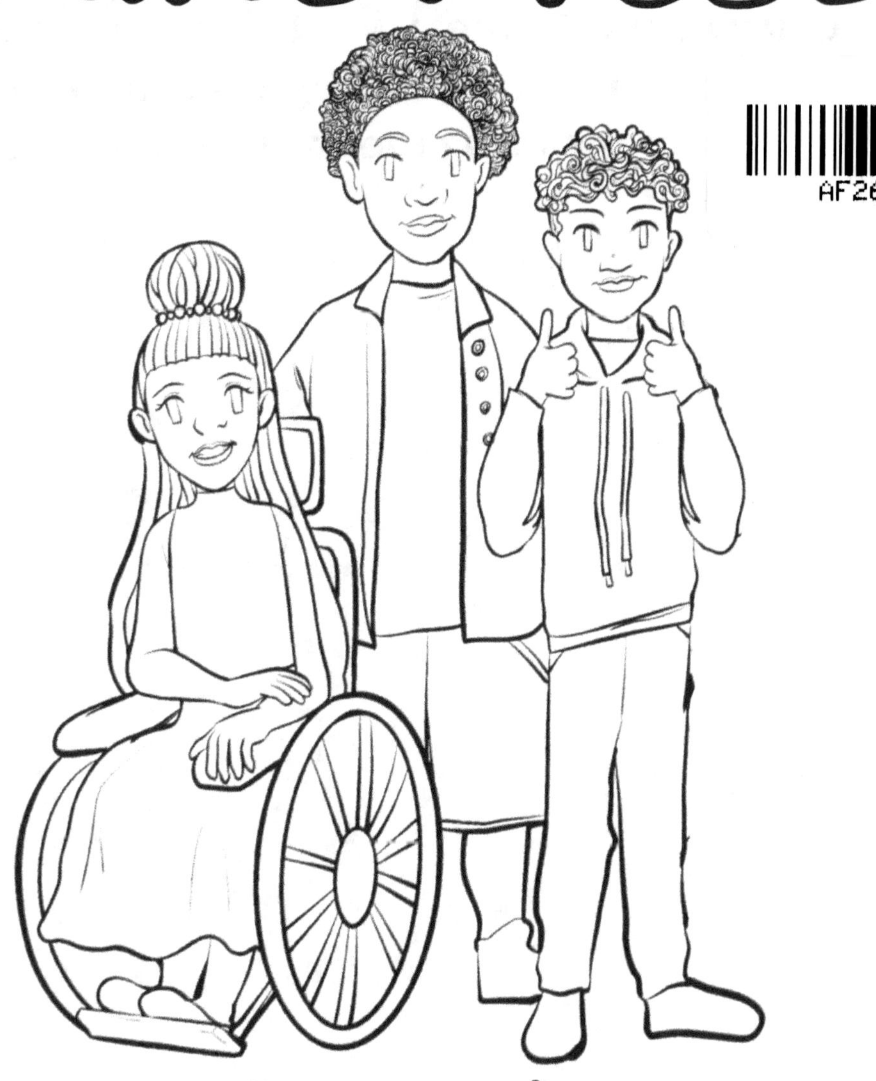

Written by
Denera McCullough

Dedication

This book is dedicated to my family and friends who continuously support me. I want to say a special thank you to my children, nieces, nephews, and childhood friends, for inspiring me to create this book.

This book belongs to:

____

"HAIR, HAIR
I LOVE MY HAIR.
I LOVE THE
STYLE I CHOOSE
TO WEAR!"

- Denera McCullough

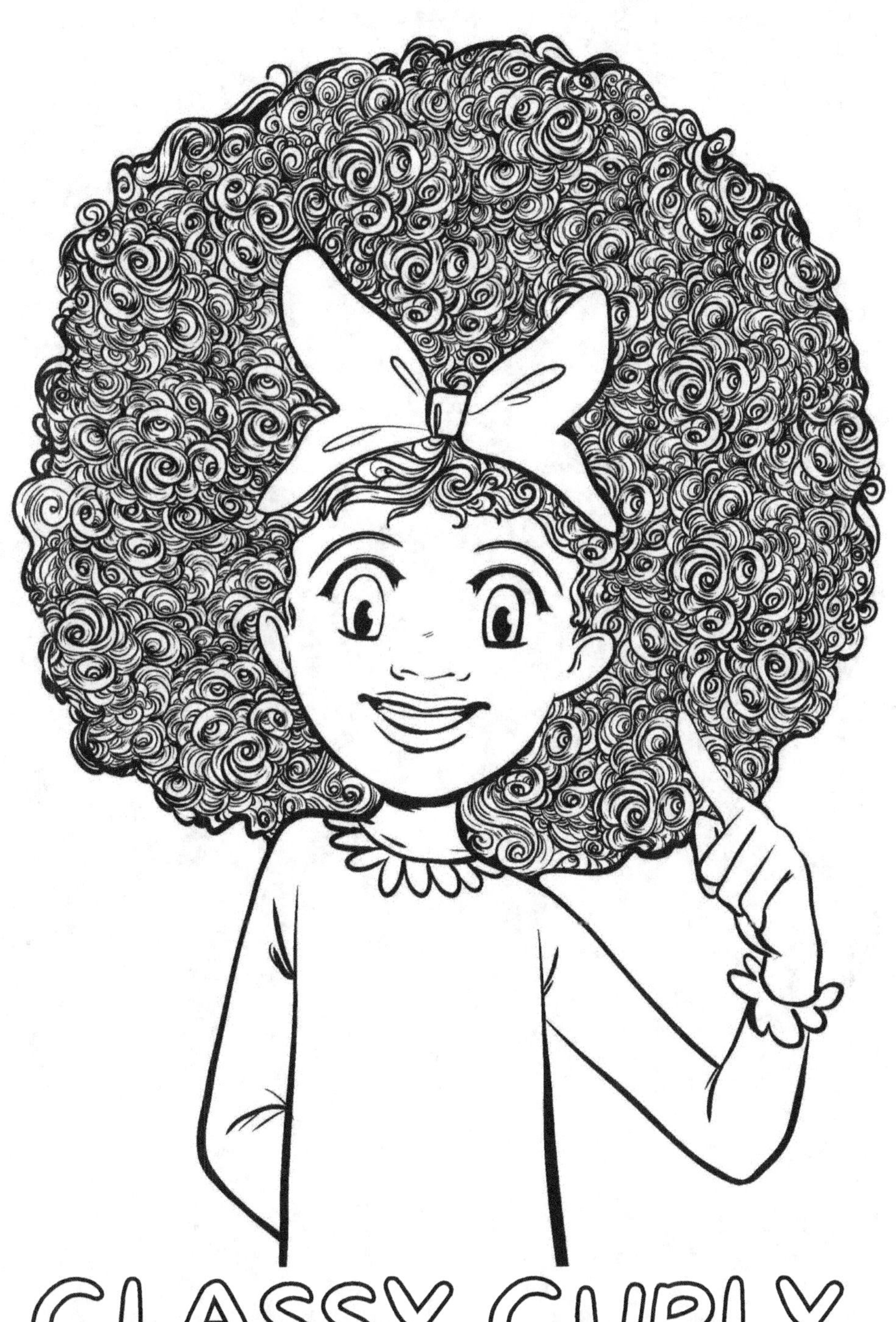

CLASSY CURLY

"HAIR, HAIR, I LOVE MY HAIR.
I LOVE THE STYLE I CHOOSE TO
WEAR!"

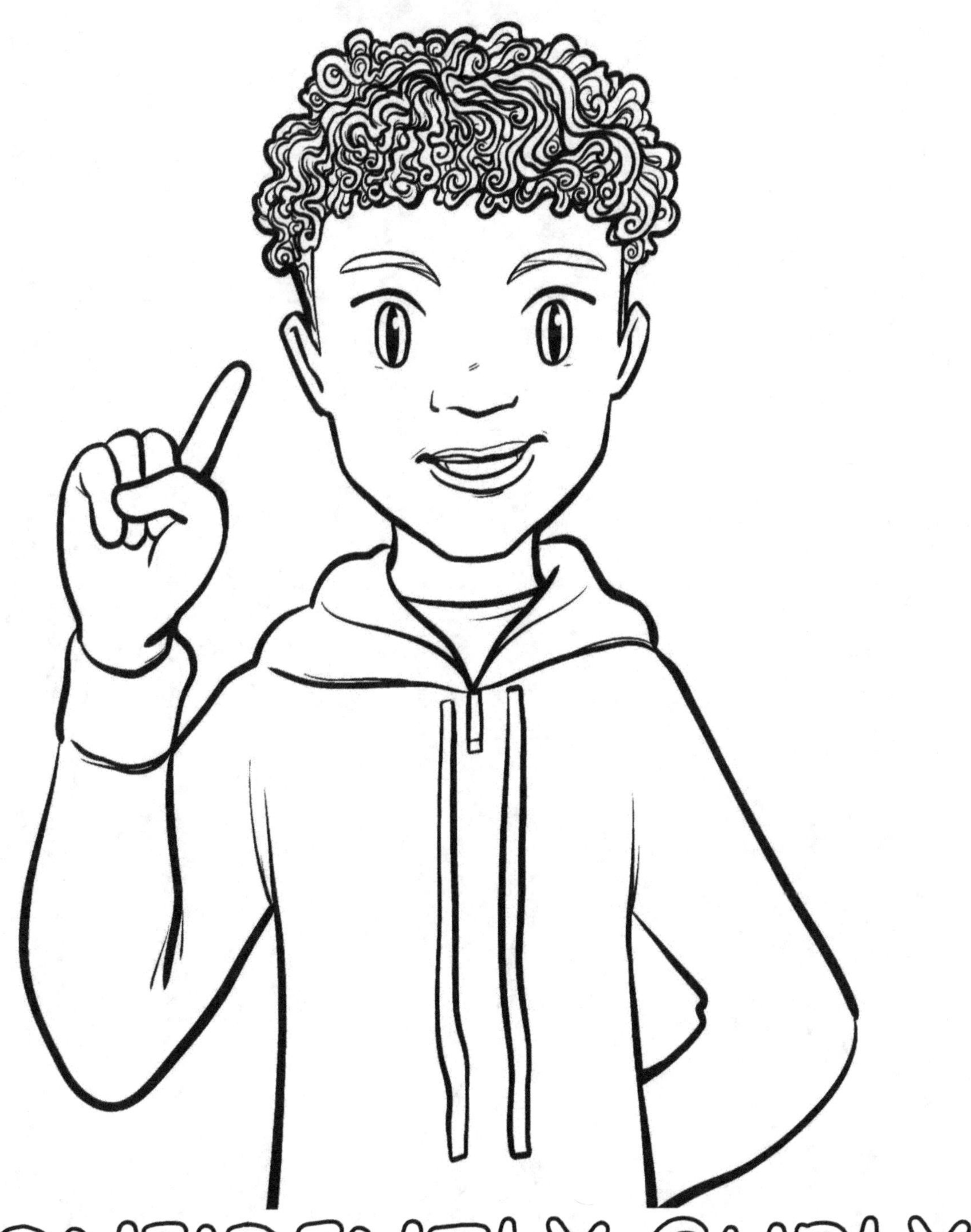

CONFIDENTLY CURLY

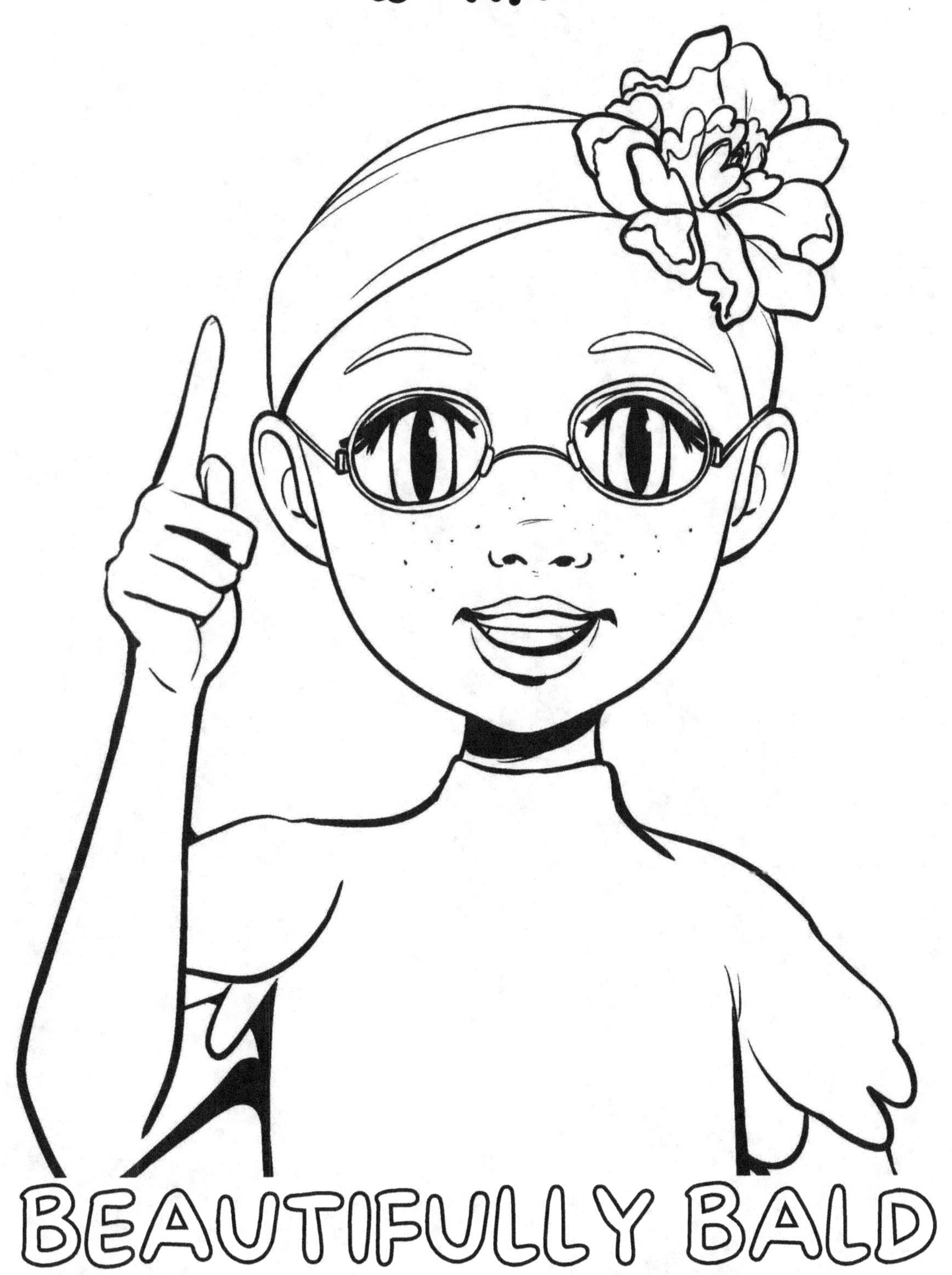

"HAIR, HAIR, I LOVE MY HAIR.
I LOVE THE STYLE I CHOOSE TO
WEAR!"
BEAUTIFULLY BALD

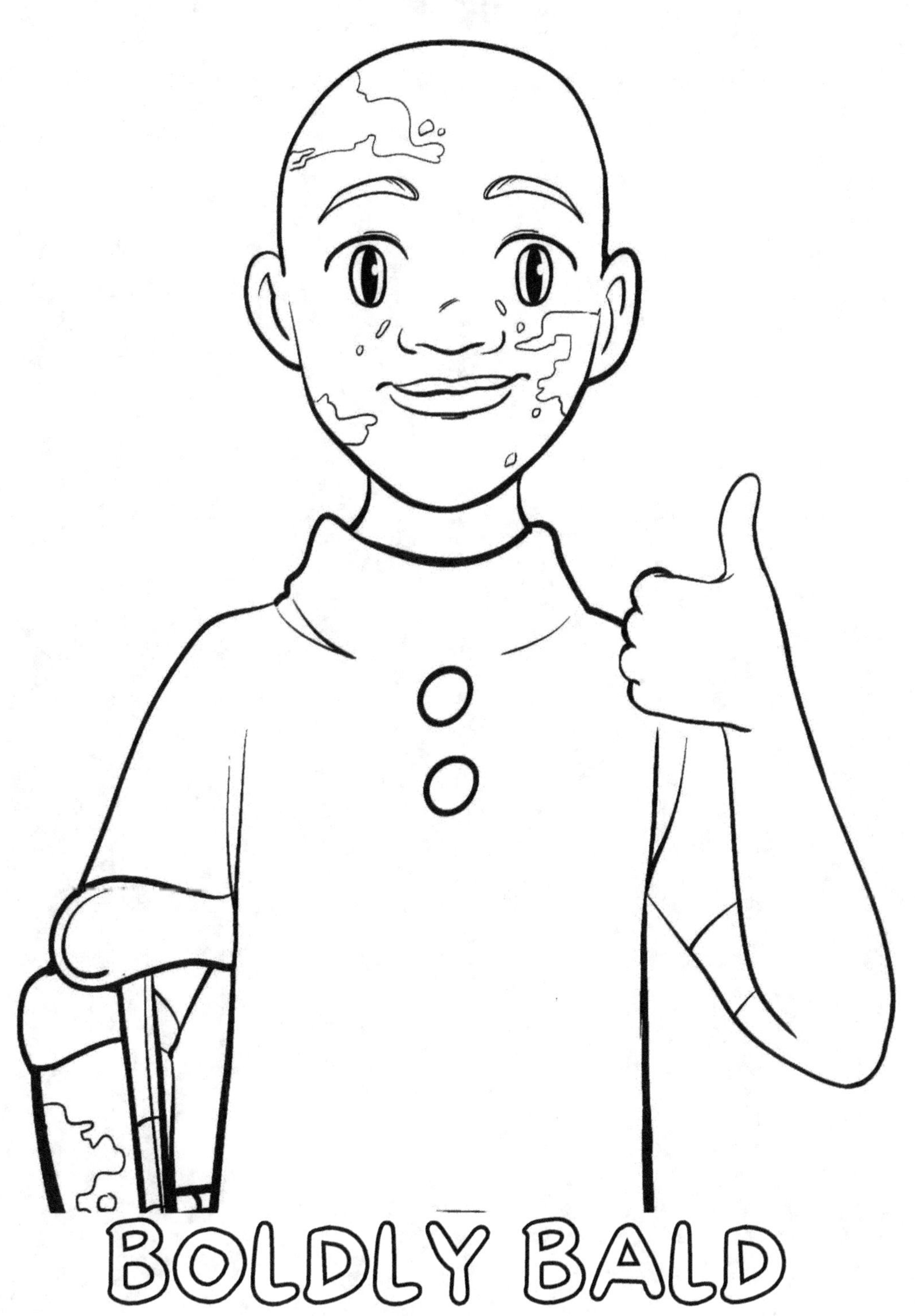

"HAIR, HAIR, I LOVE MY HAIR. I LOVE THE STYLE I CHOOSE TO WEAR!"
BOLDLY BALD

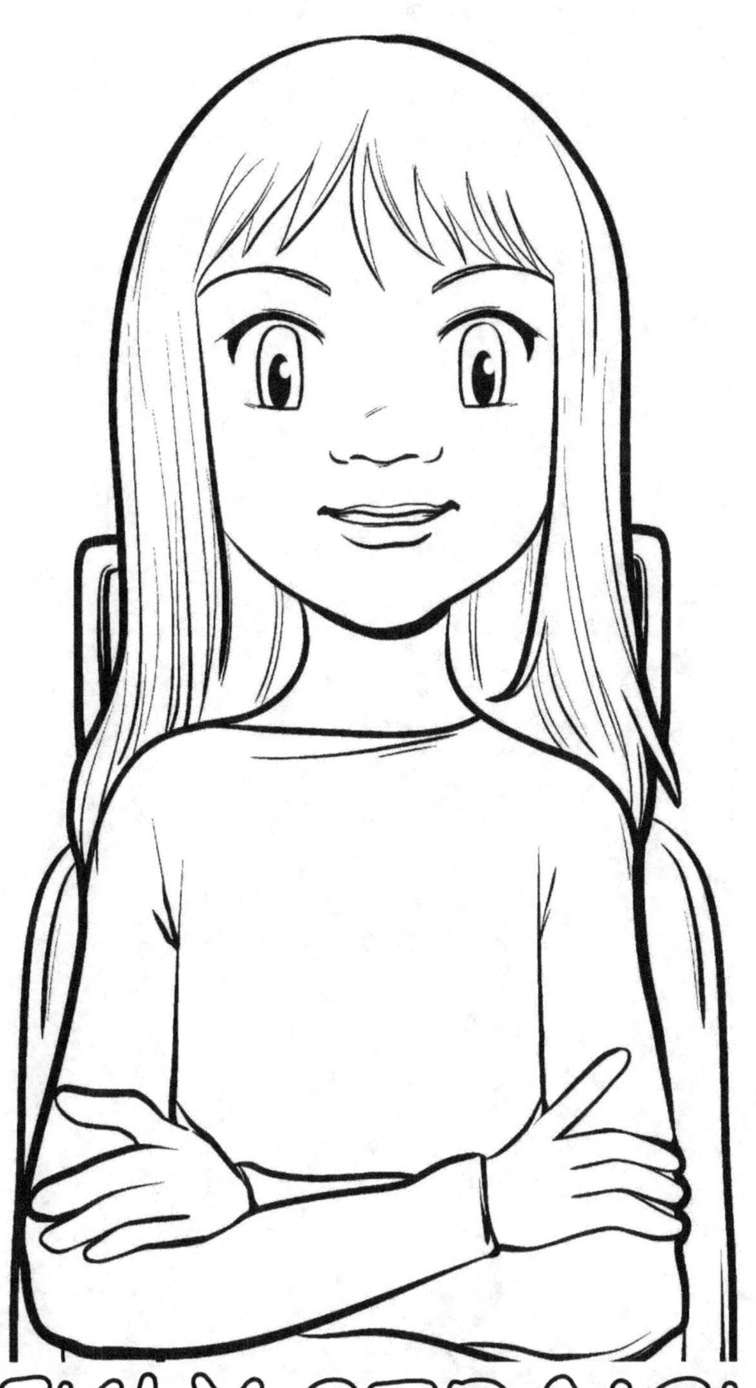

SLEEKLY STRAIGHT

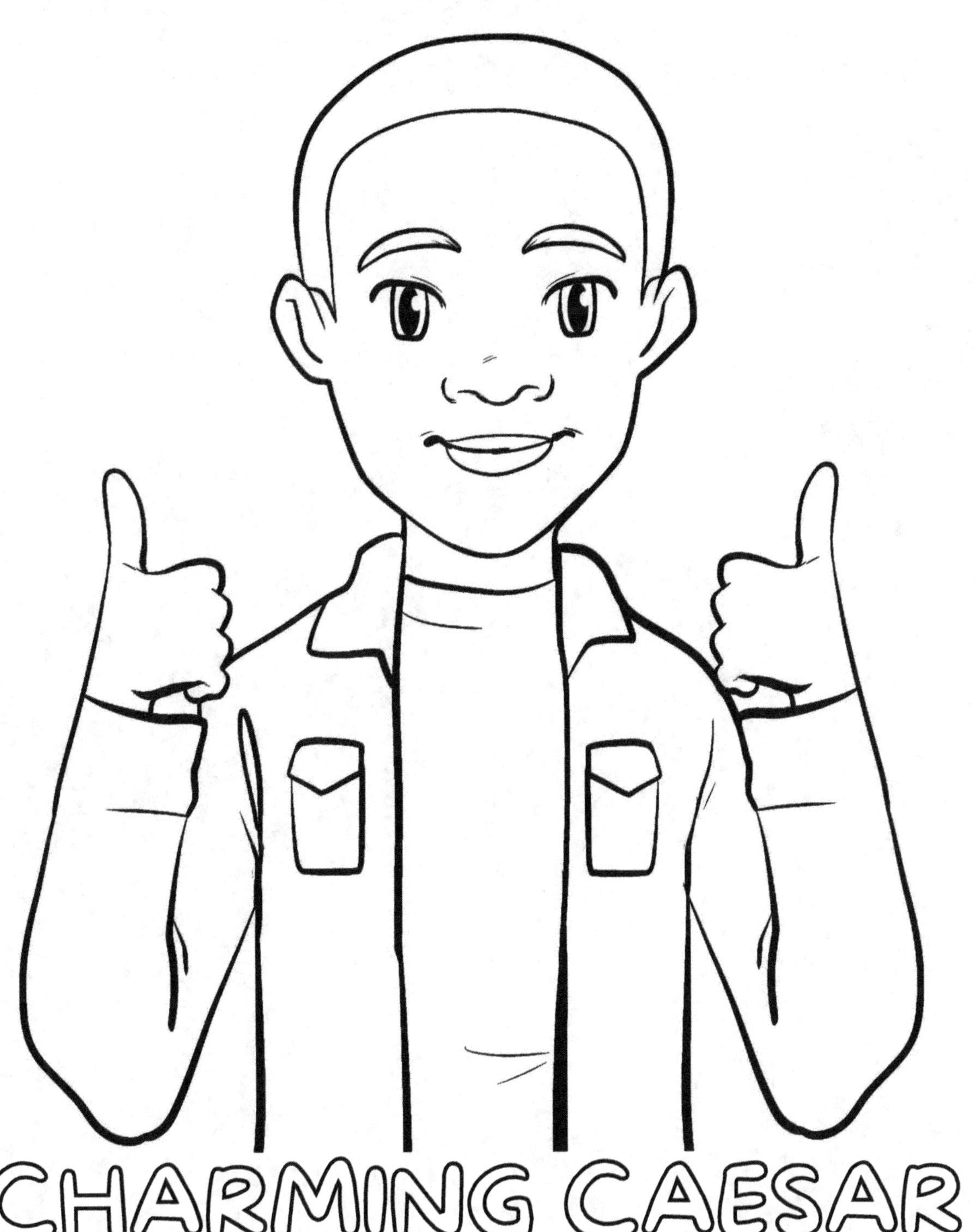

"HAIR, HAIR, I LOVE MY HAIR.
I LOVE THE STYLE I CHOOSE TO
WEAR!"

CHARMING CAESAR

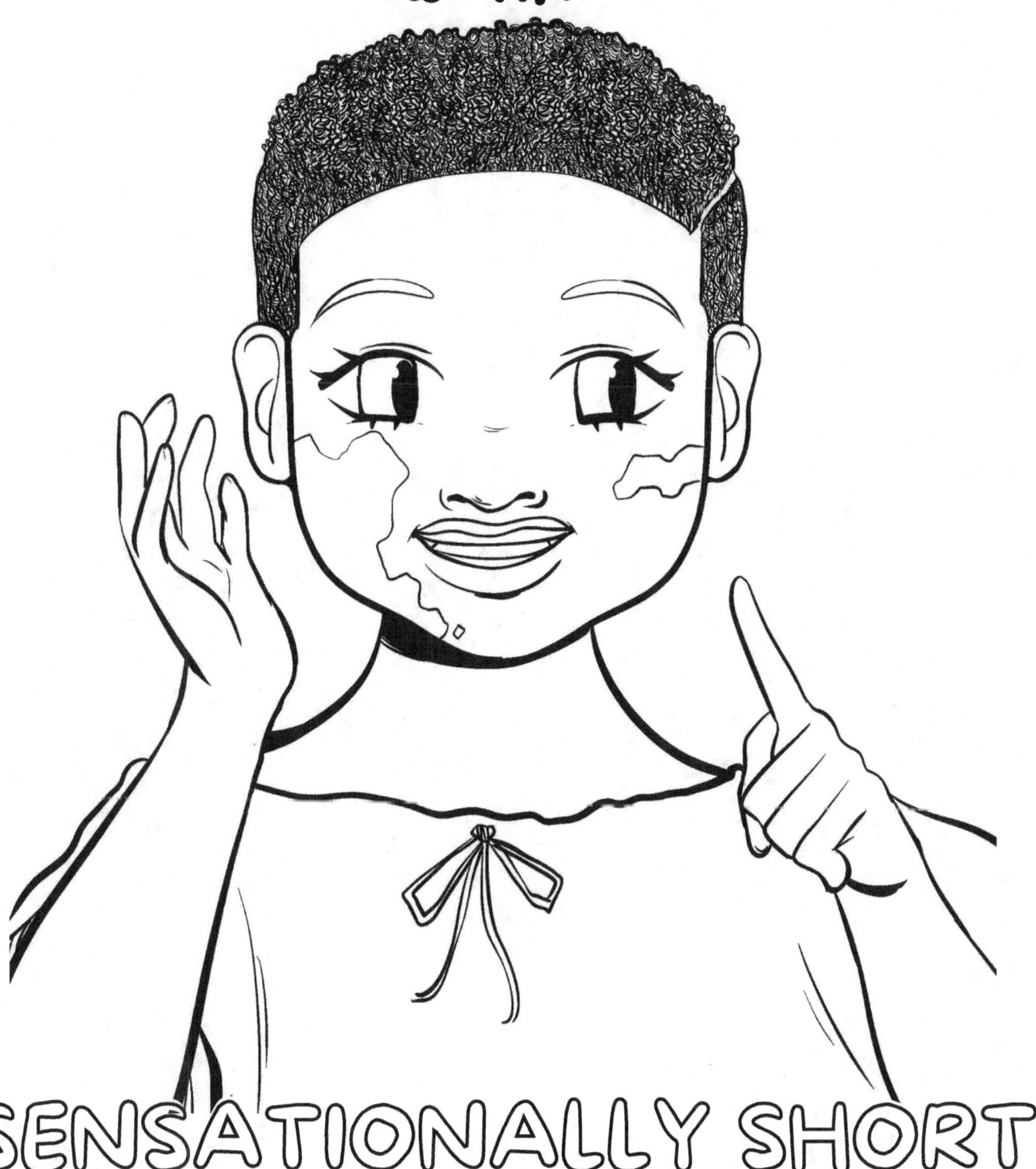
"HAIR, HAIR, I LOVE MY HAIR.
I LOVE THE STYLE I CHOOSE TO
WEAR!"
SENSATIONALLY SHORT

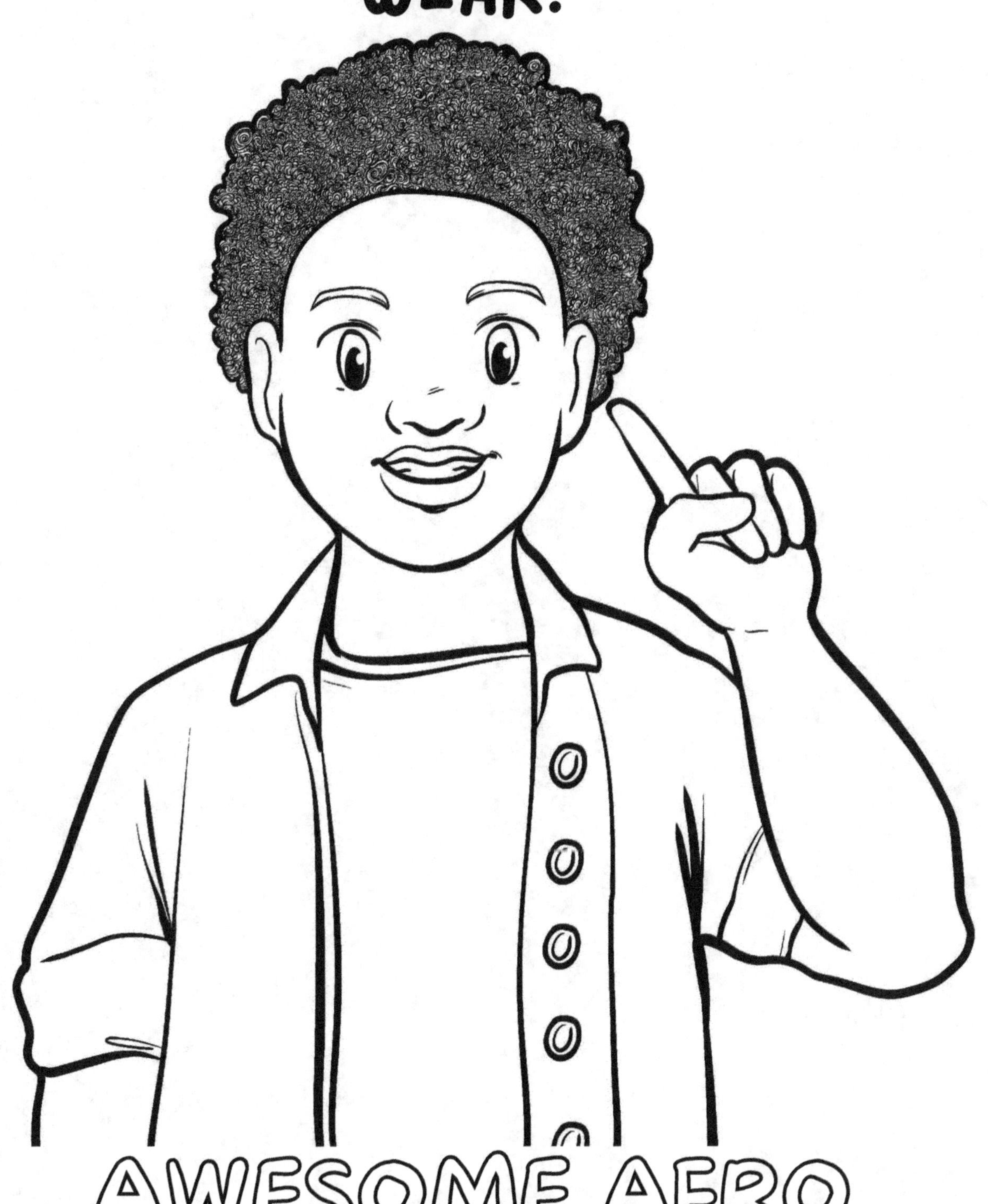

"HAIR, HAIR, I LOVE MY HAIR. I LOVE THE STYLE I CHOOSE TO WEAR!"
AWESOME AFRO

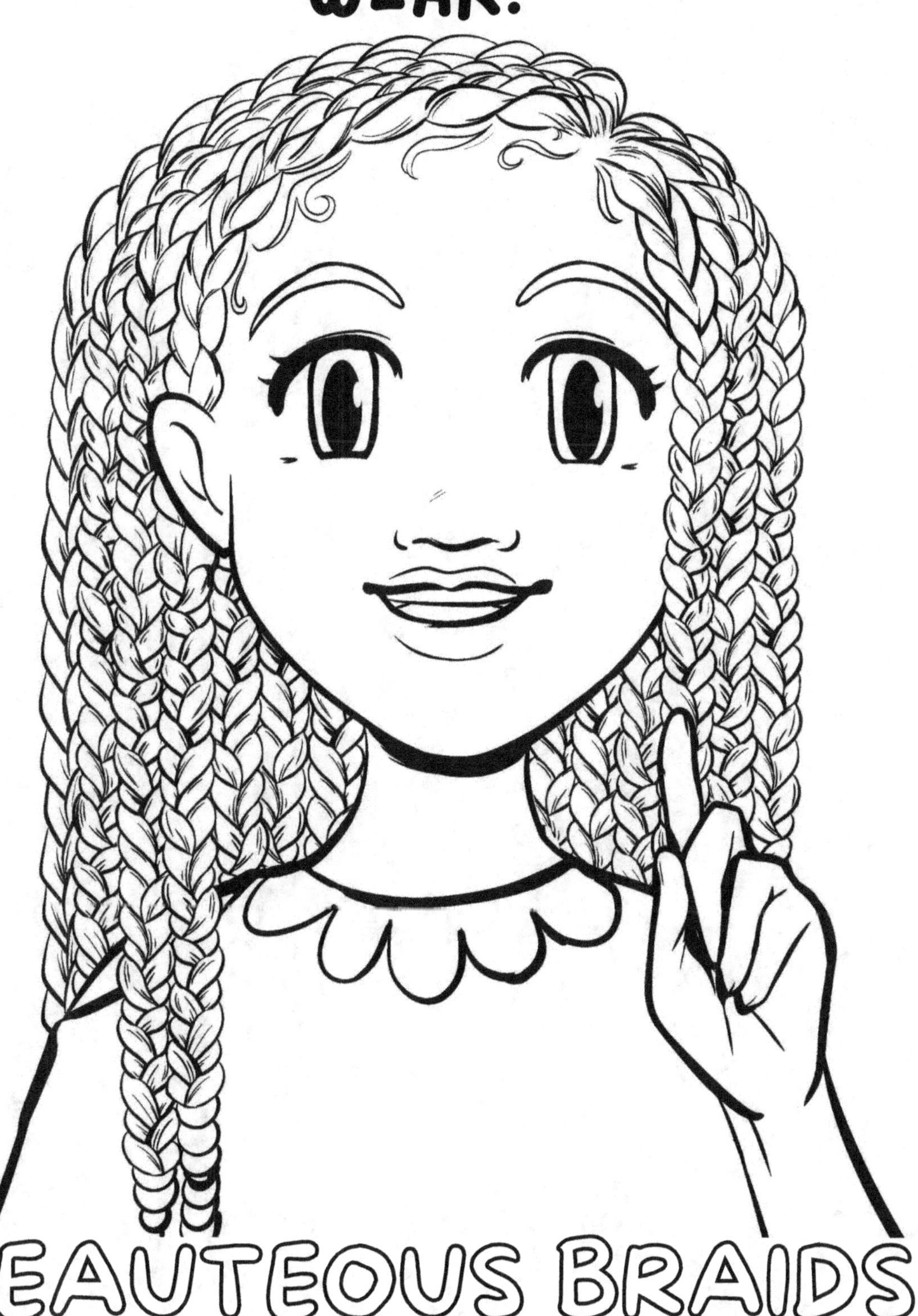

"HAIR, HAIR, I LOVE MY HAIR.
I LOVE THE STYLE I CHOOSE TO WEAR!"

BEAUTEOUS BRAIDS

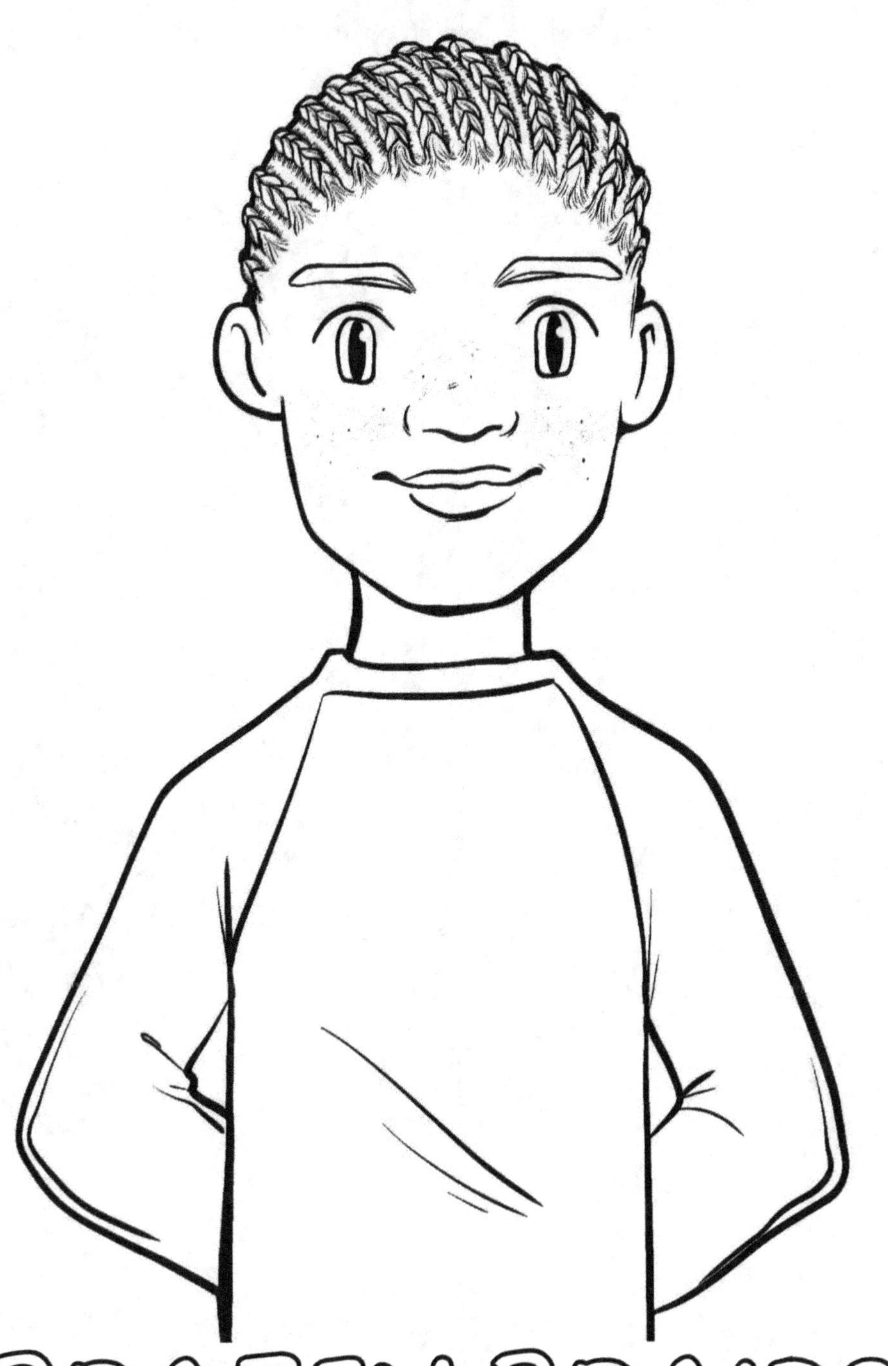

BRAZEN BRAIDS

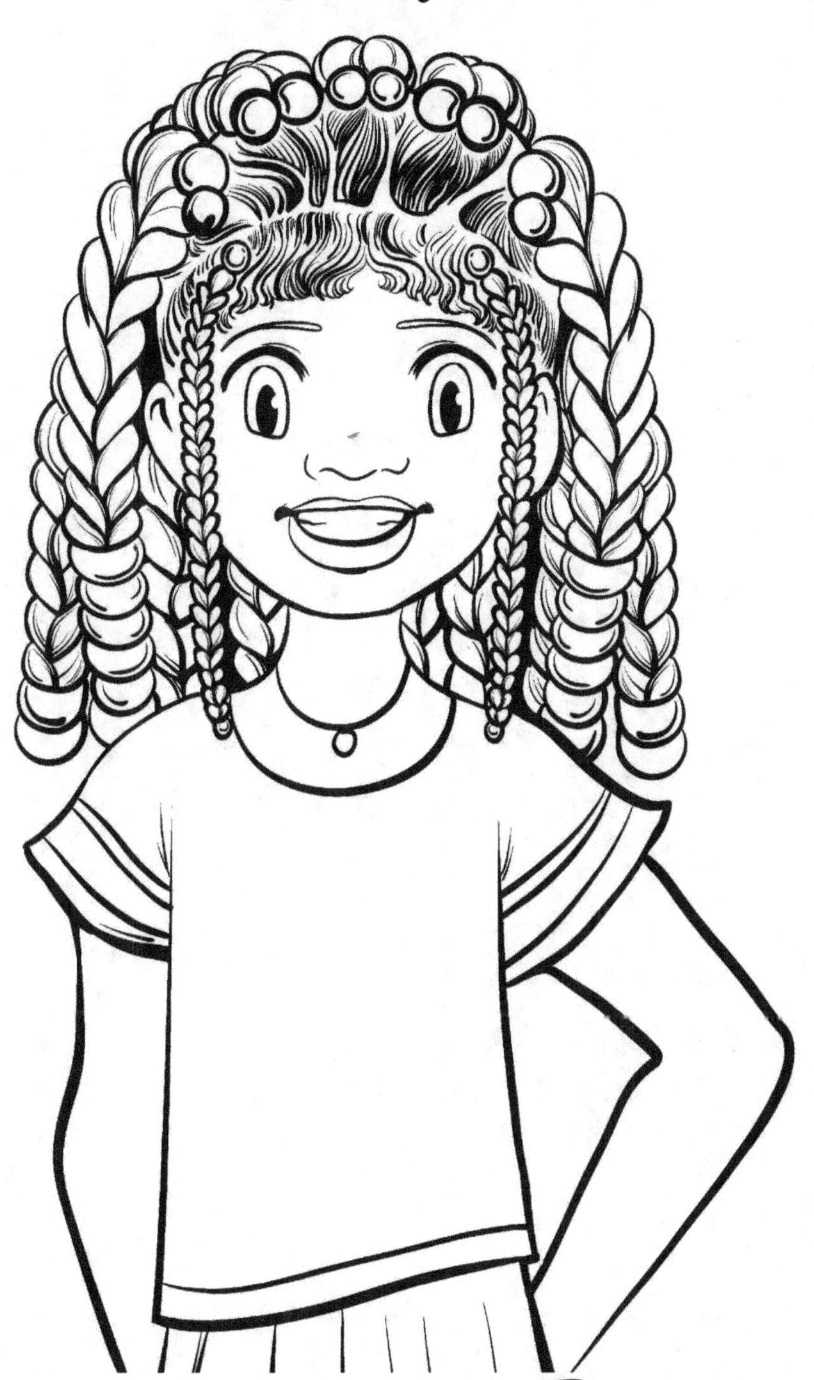

BODACIOUS BRAIDS

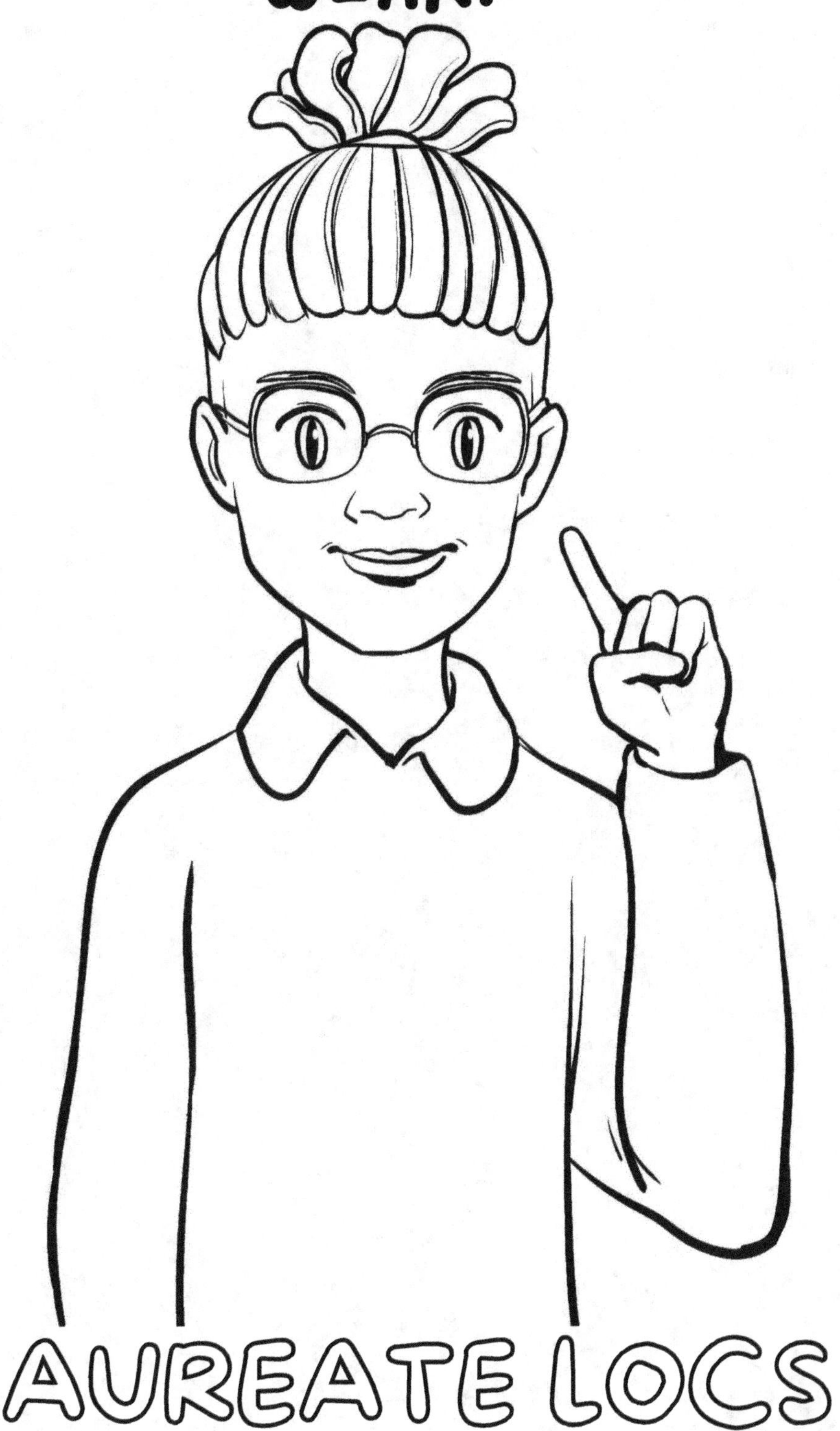

"HAIR, HAIR, I LOVE MY HAIR. I LOVE THE STYLE I CHOOSE TO WEAR!"
LAUREATE LOCS

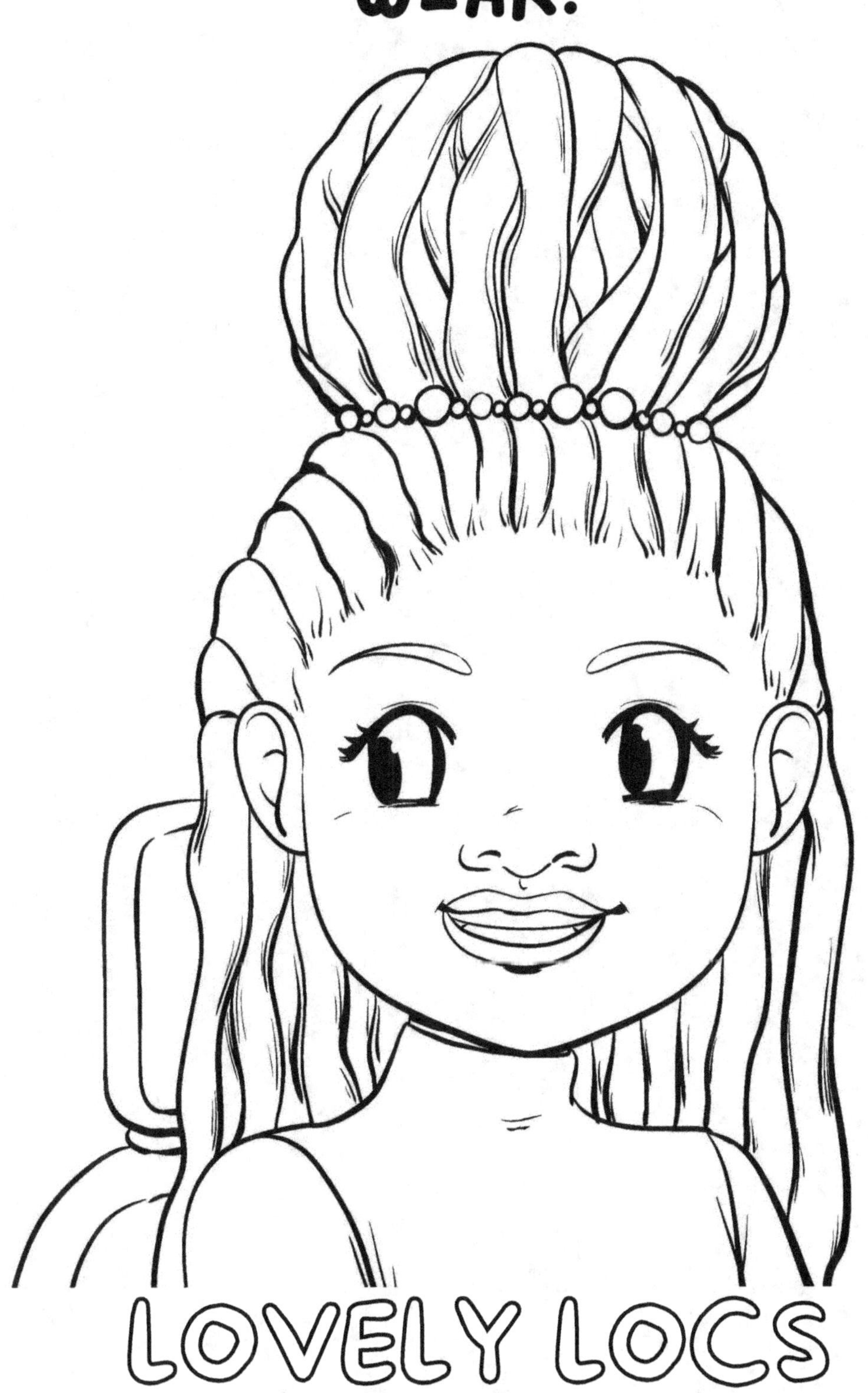

"HAIR, HAIR, I LOVE MY HAIR.
I LOVE THE STYLE I CHOOSE TO
WEAR!"

LOVELY LOCS

DRAW A SELFIE

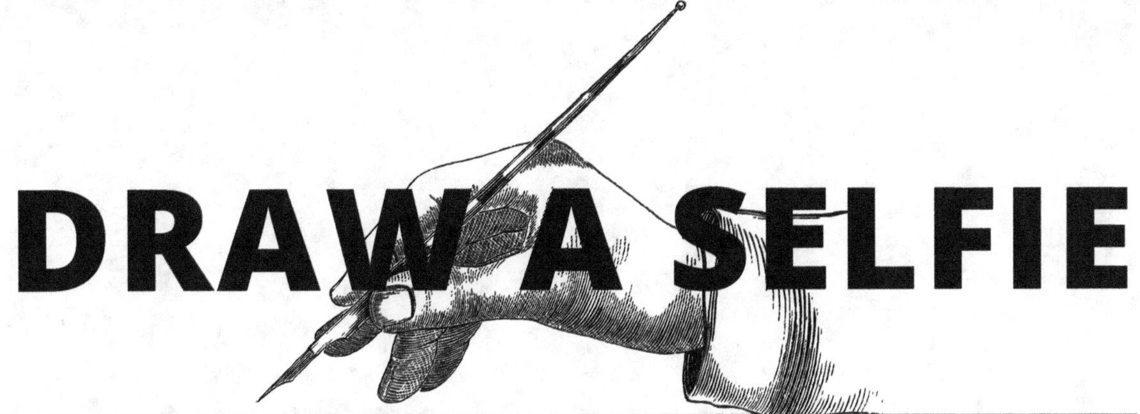

Draw a picture of yourself.

ALL ABOUT MY HAIR!

Draw your 4 favorite hairstyles.

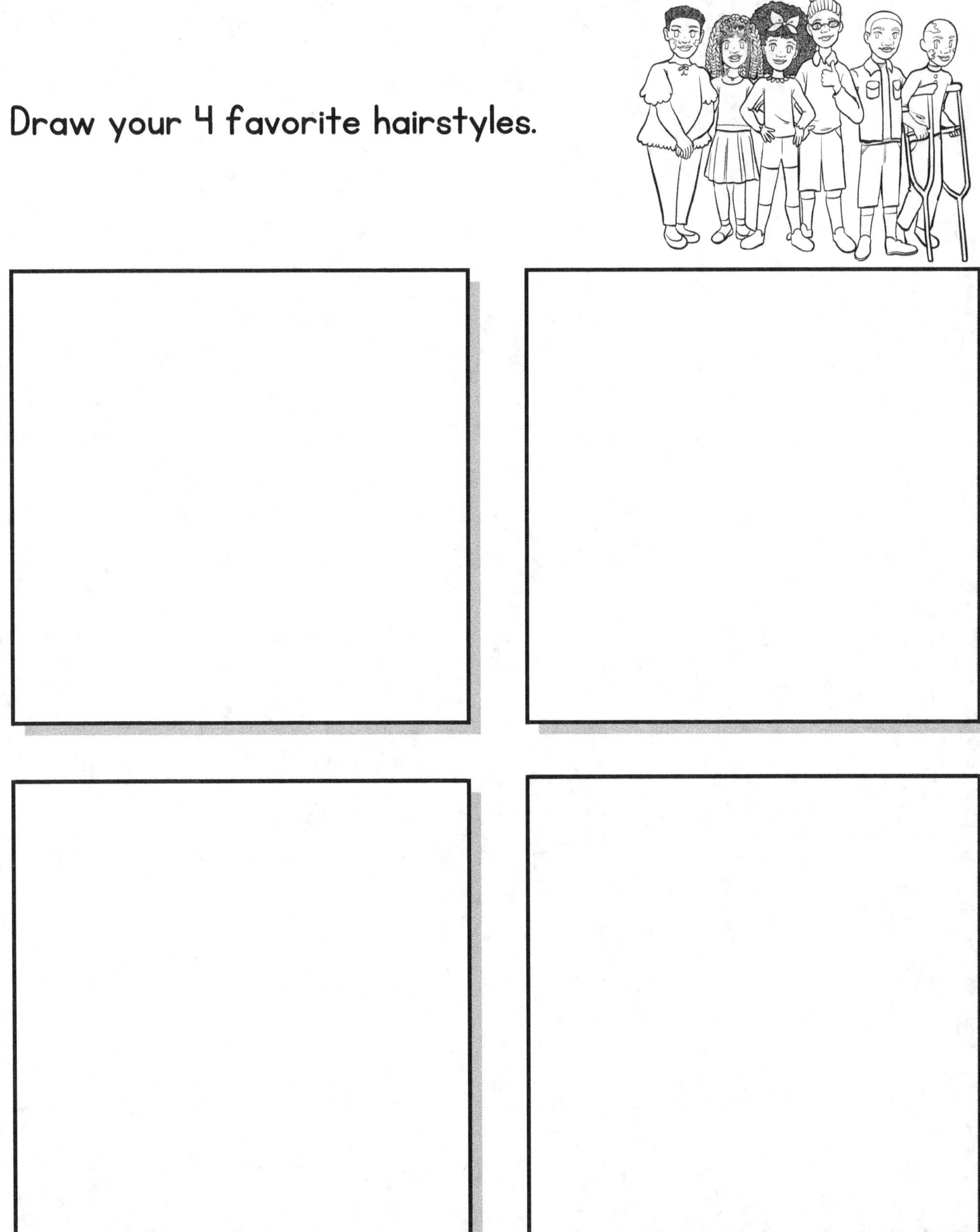

Word Search

```
B  T  W  A  N  T  A  S  T  I  C  V
M  R  A  Y  H  E  H  P  F  U  L  F
O  N  A  E  C  O  I  L  Y  A  O  B
H  I  E  I  Z  P  H  U  T  N  W  I
A  M  S  D  D  T  I  D  K  P  C  W
W  C  S  F  I  S  T  E  L  X  U  D
K  A  Q  C  L  L  O  C  O  V  T  E
U  L  A  O  A  K  P  E  W  A  J  T
L  M  C  S  Y  I  E  G  C  R  H  I
U  O  R  F  O  N  S  B  E  A  D  S
P  A  D  V  L  D  F  X  M  N  H  X
S  U  O  R  E  C  U  R  L  Y  T  S
```

HI TOP　　　　**FRO**　　　　**BEADS**

MOHAWK　　　**BRAIDS**　　　**LOW CUT**

MAZING FUN

Can you help Tony find his friend Ramon?

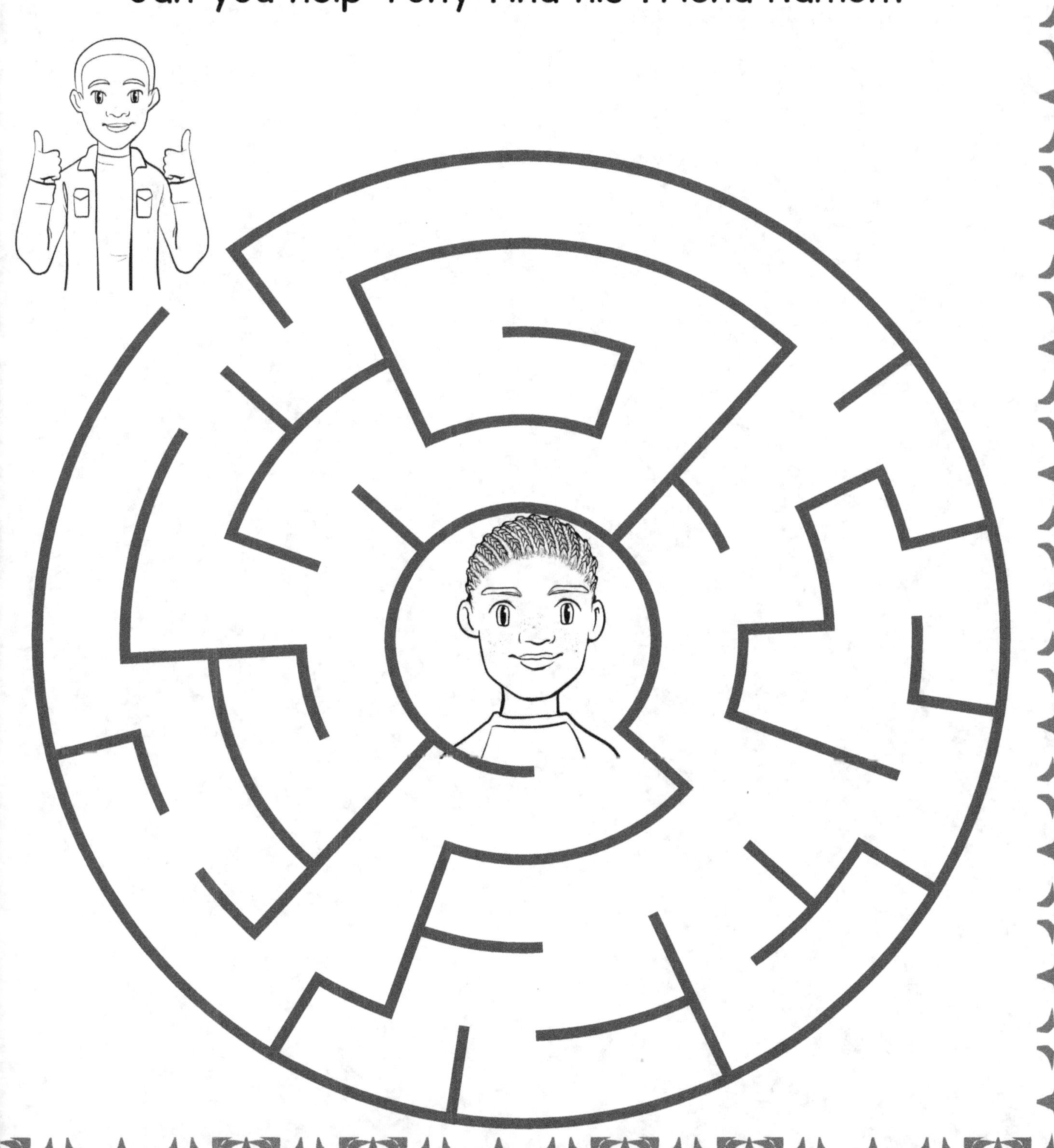

I AM...
Word Search

```
B T W O R T H Y T I C V
G S A Y H E Z P F U L T
R N U E C O A L Y D O N
A G N O R T S U E N W E
T M S D I Q D V D P C I
E C U F P T O N L X U L
F A N C D L I C O V T I
U L I O E K M B W A J S
L M Q K V I E G M R H E
U O U F O N S B E A D R
P N E V A R B X M N H X
S M A R T C O O L Y T S
```

WORTHY   BRAVE   COOL   KIND

RESILIENT   AMBITIOUS   GRATEFUL

LOVED   STRONG   SMART   UNIQUE

MAZING FUN

Get Noah to the finish line.

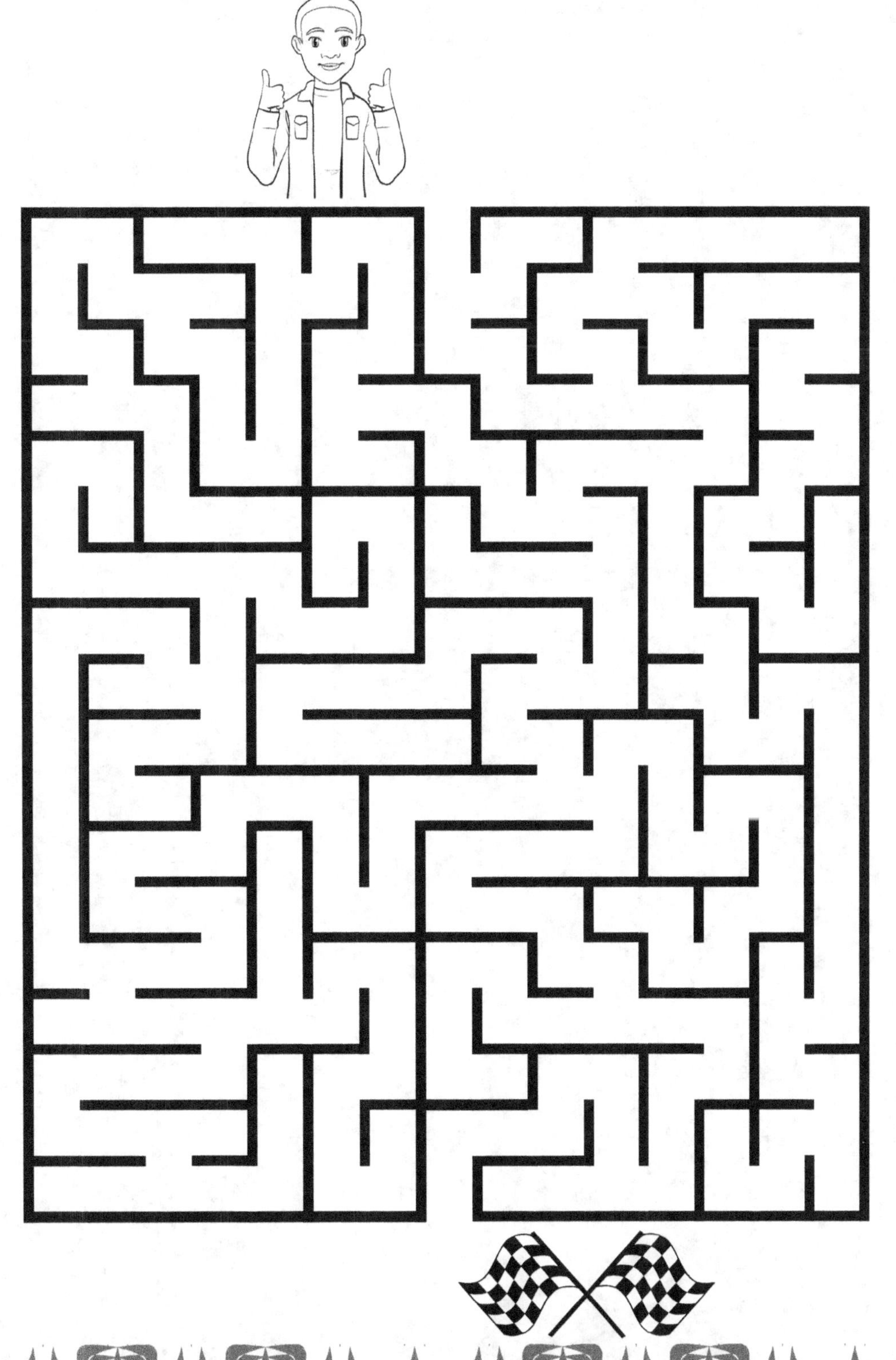

WHAT DO I LIKE ABOUT MY HAIR?

Ex: I like that my hair can have cool designs.

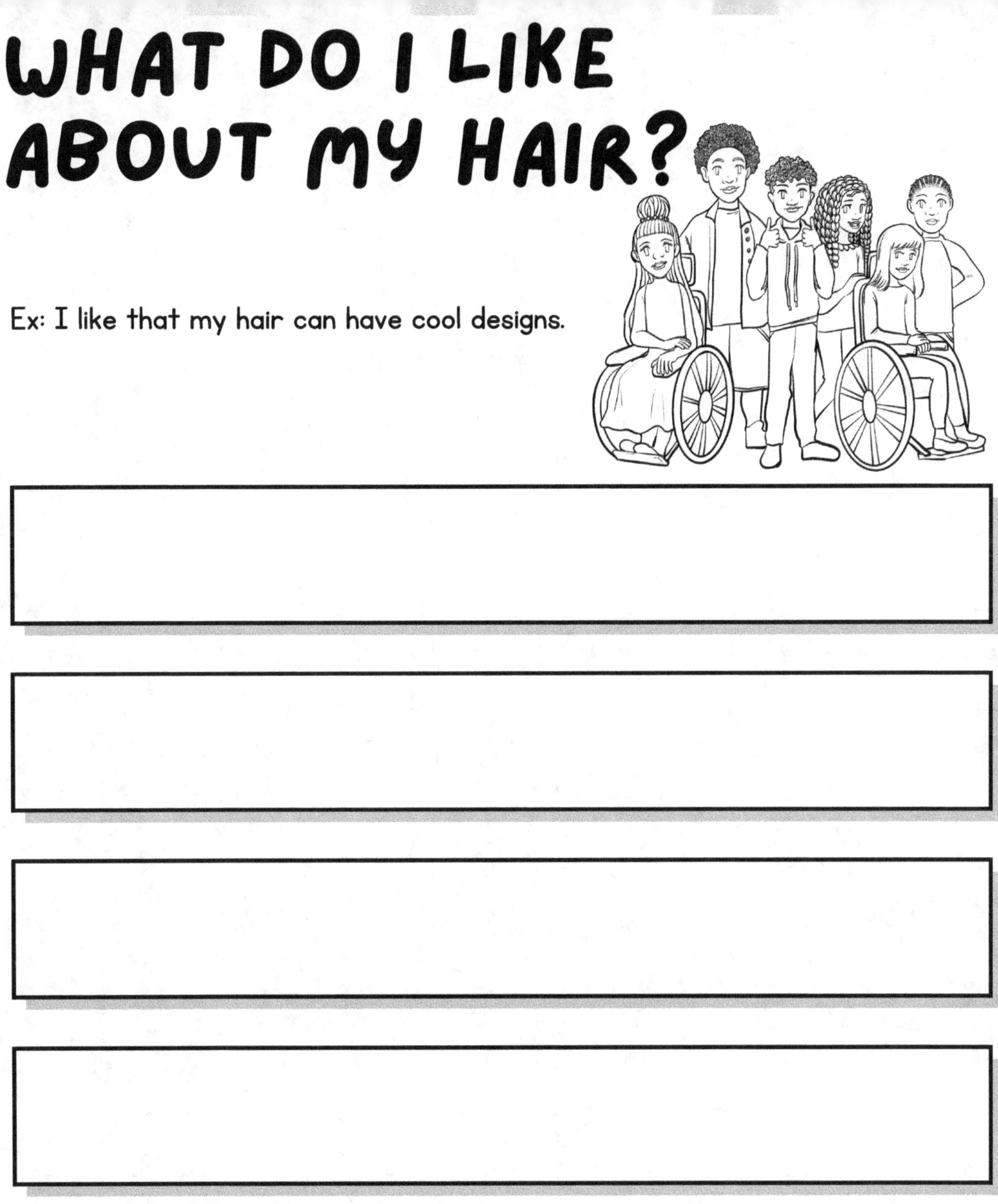

Word Search

```
B T W A N T A S T I C V
E Y A Y H E L P F U L F
A N V E C B A L D A F B
U I E V I P I U T N A I
T M S D A T U D K P D W
I C S F I D A E L X E D
F A Q C L L O C P V R E
U L A O A K I E D A J T
L M C S Y I X G P R H I
U S W G O N S B E A D S
P A D V L D F X M N H X
S U O R E C U R L Y T S
```

BALD   **LOCS**   **FADE**

SHAPE UP   **WAVES**   **CURLY**

MAZING FUN

Who can get to the bike first?

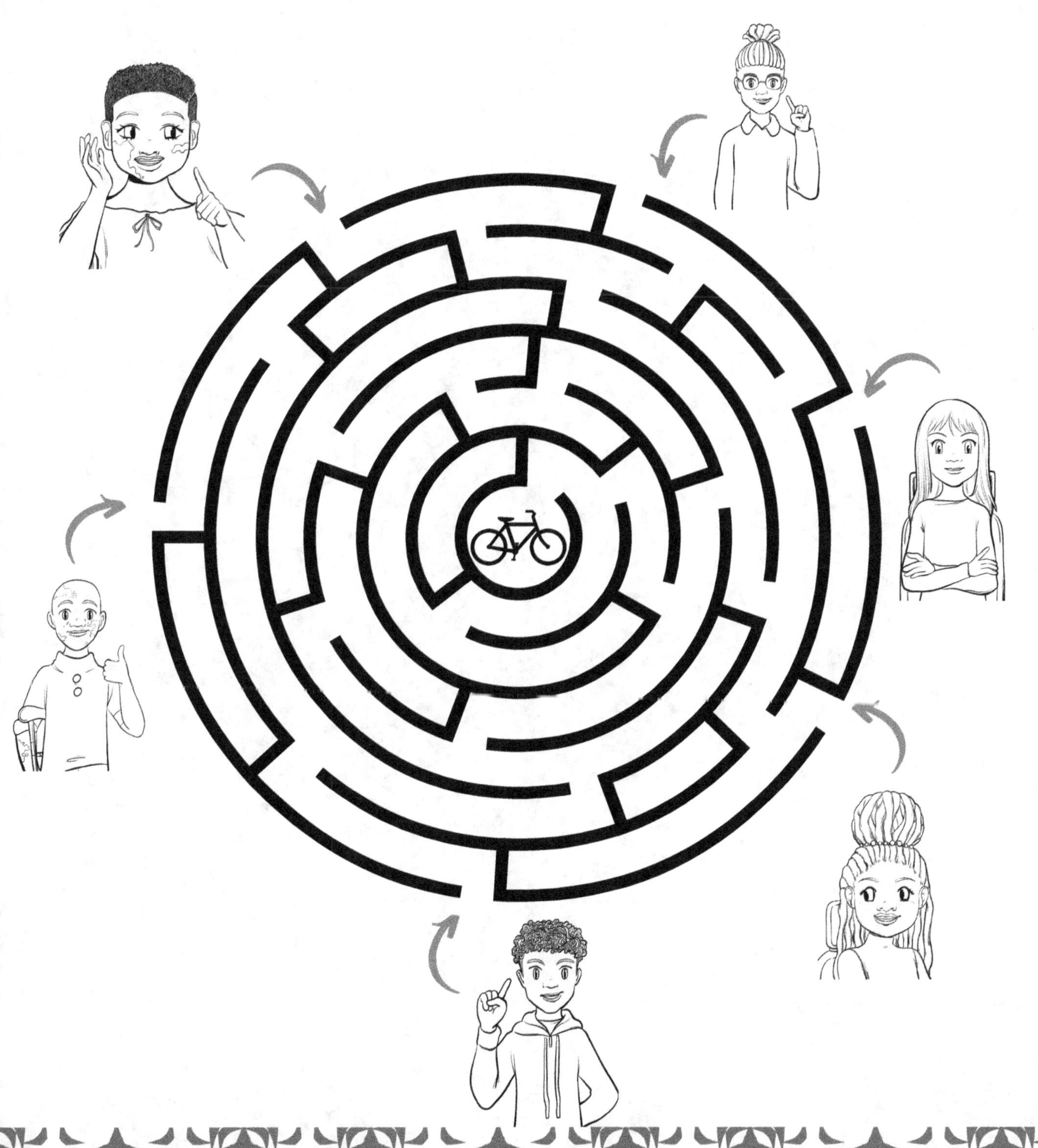

I AM...
Word Search

E T W E V I T A E R C V
X S A Y H E L P F U L I
C N Z E S T Y L Y D O R
E G N O R N S U E N W T
P M S D I A D V D P C U
T C U F P I O N L X U O
I A N C D L I C O V T U
O L I O E A M B W A J S
N M Q K Y V E N O U G H
A O U F O N Z B E A D R
L N E C I T S A T N A F
C A P A B L E O L Y T S

ZESTY   VIRTUOUS   VALIANT

CAPABLE   FANTASTIC   HELPFUL

EXCEPTIONAL   ENOUGH CREATIVE

MAZING FUN

Who can reach Deniyah first?

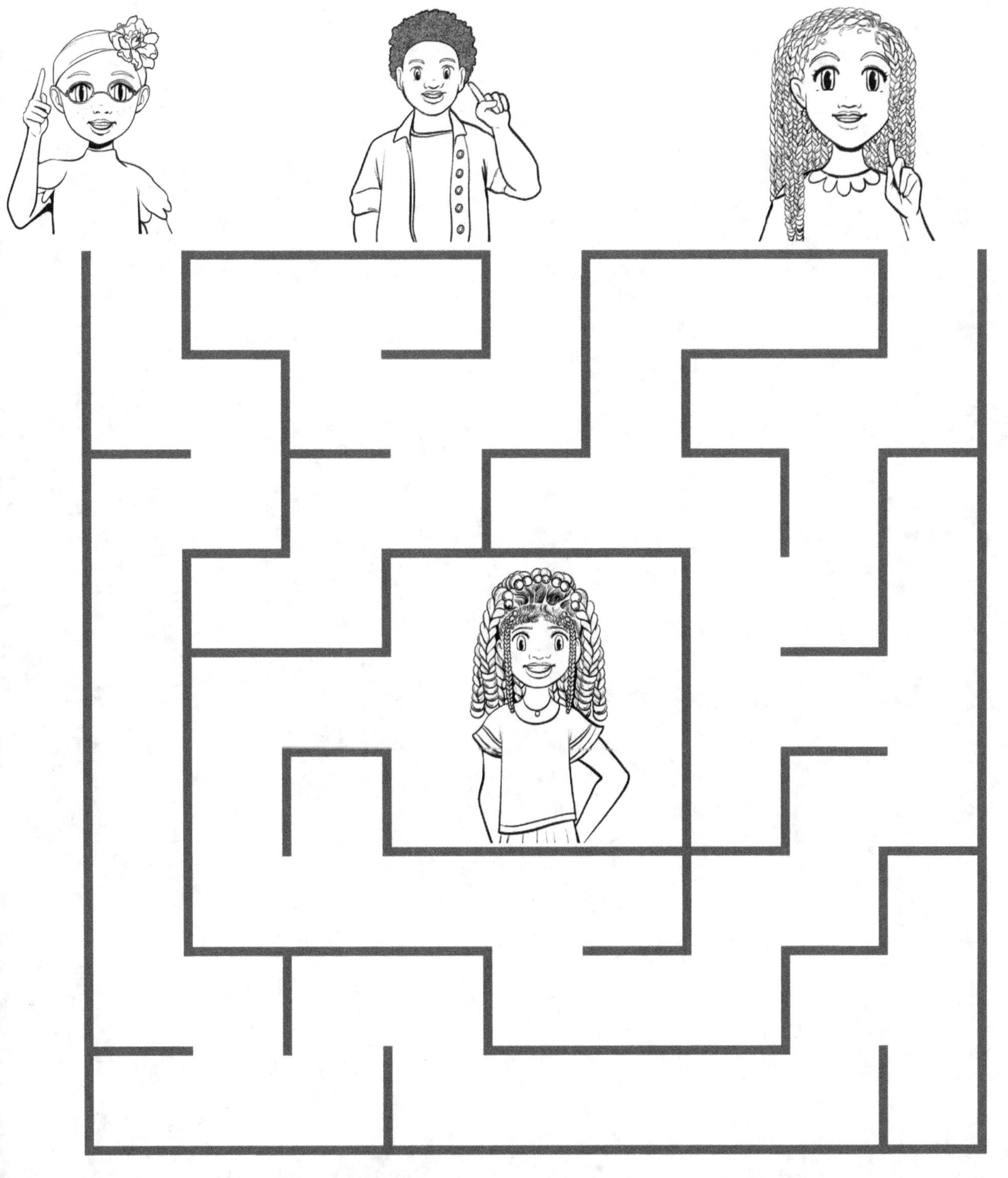

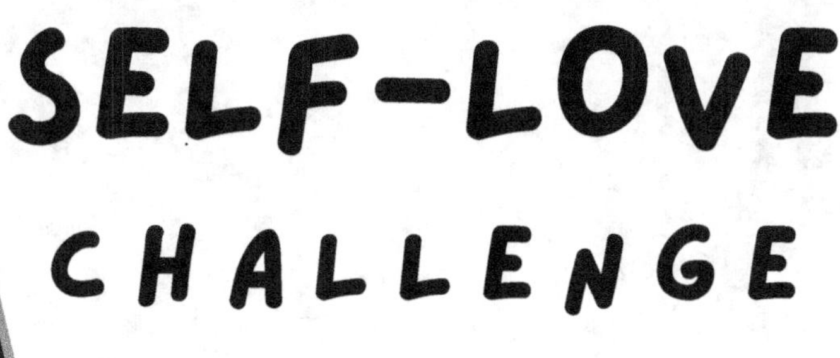

SELF-LOVE
CHALLENGE

Look in the mirror and say out loud everyday...

I am brave.

I am worthy.

I define myself.

I am ONE of a kind.

I love myself.

I am confident.

I am strong.

I am limitless.

I can only be myself.

ROLL & RESPOND

Cut along the outside. Fold in the flaps. Secure with tape.
Roll the die and according to the result, talk about the topic.

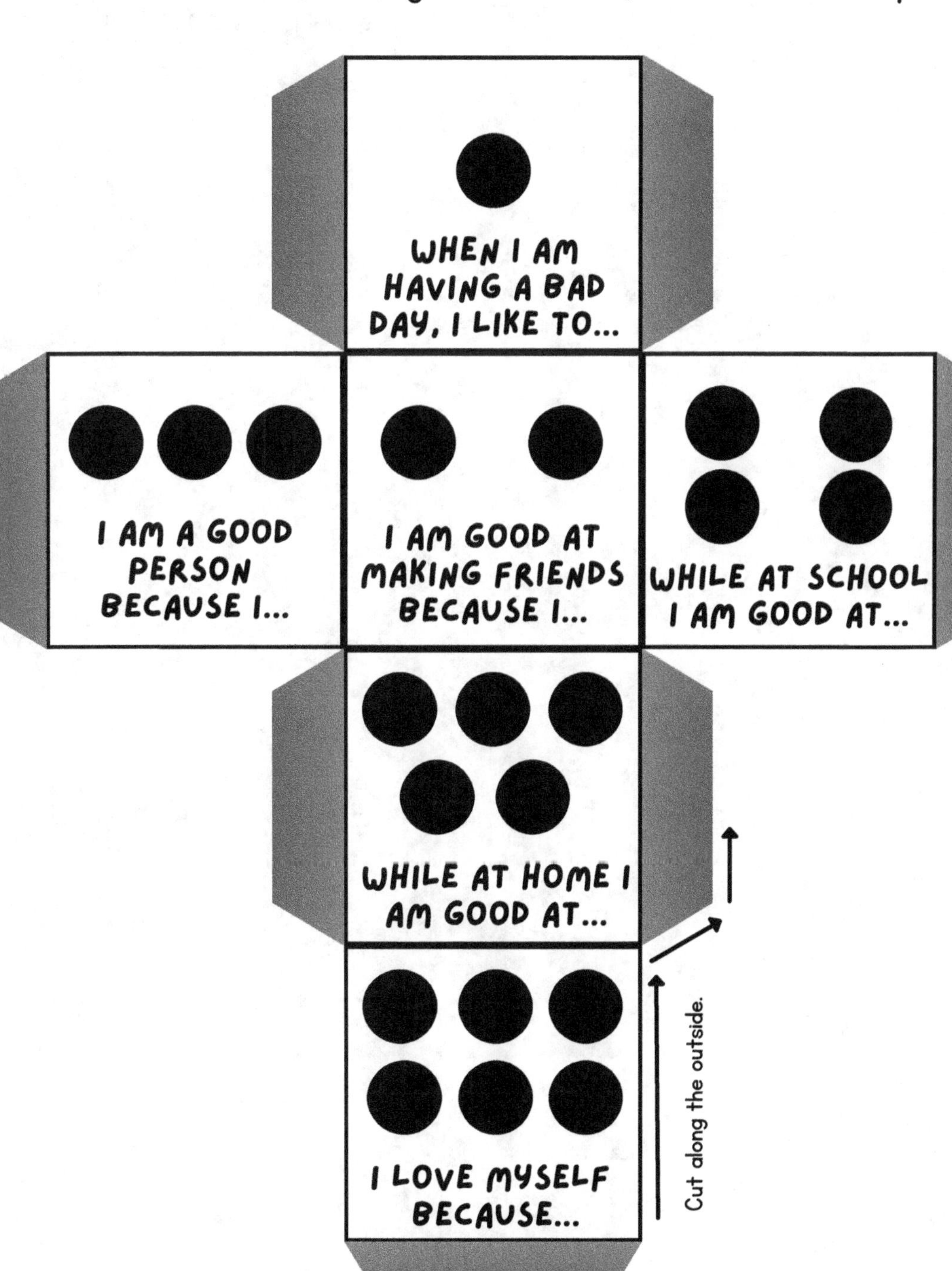

I AM ...

EXCEPTIONAL FAIR FUN

CALM CARING

ZESTY VIRTUOUS KIND

VALIANT RESILIENT

AMBITIOUS STRONG BOLD

BRAVE CAPABLE

CREATIVE ME WORTHY

BRIGHT GRATEFUL

ROYAL SMART HELPFUL

AWESOME ENOUGH

LIMITLESS

CONFIDENT HONEST

GLOSSARY

Ambitious – having or showing a strong desire and determination to succeed

Beauteous – very attractive

Beautiful – very attractive

Bodacious – remarkable; bold

Bold – courageous; brave

Brave – not afraid

Brazen – no shame

Capable – able to do things

Charming – likable

Classy – of high quality; stylish

Confident – proud; having trust

Creative – able to make or do something new or with imagination

Exceptional – very good; memorable

Fantastic – very good; amazing

Laureate – an honor for outstanding creativity

Lovely – very pretty; elegant

Resilient – able to adjust to change; succeed under pressure

Sensational – very amazing; elegant

Sleekly – smooth and glossy; stylish

Valiant – brave; heroic

Virtuous – moral excellence; loyal; nice

Worthy – important; deserving of

Zesty – sense of great joy

*Please note that there are different definitions / meanings for the same word.
This glossary is based on the context of the coloring and activity book; to display positive
reflections of different hairstyles and building self esteem.

PRODUCT REVIEW

★ ★ ★ ★ ★

LIKE THE PRODUCT?

- Spread the word
- Write/record a review
- Post about it and tag us

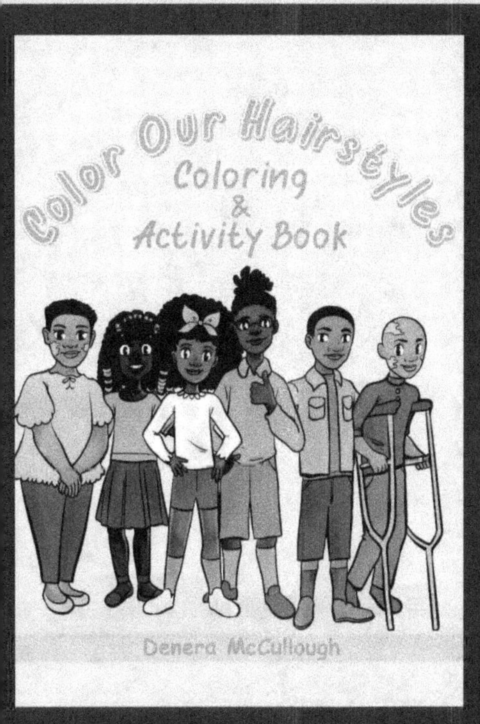

authordeneram

Author Denera M

authordeneram@gmail.com

Want more books?

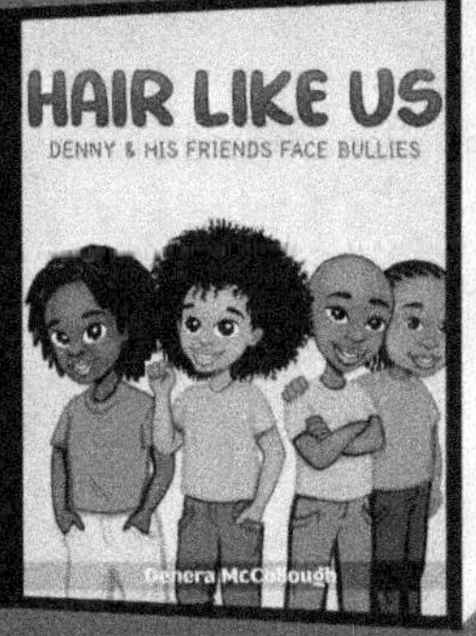

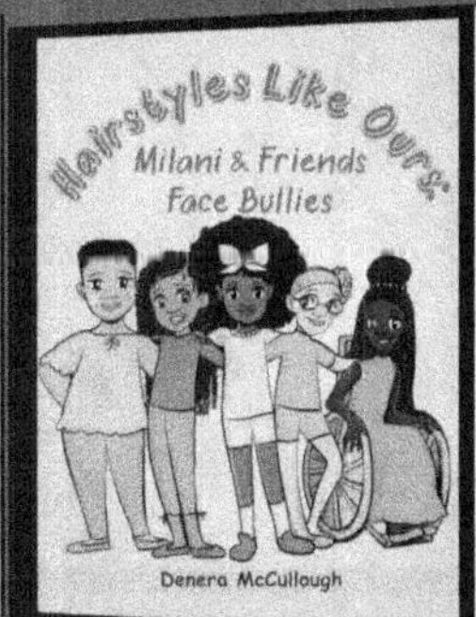

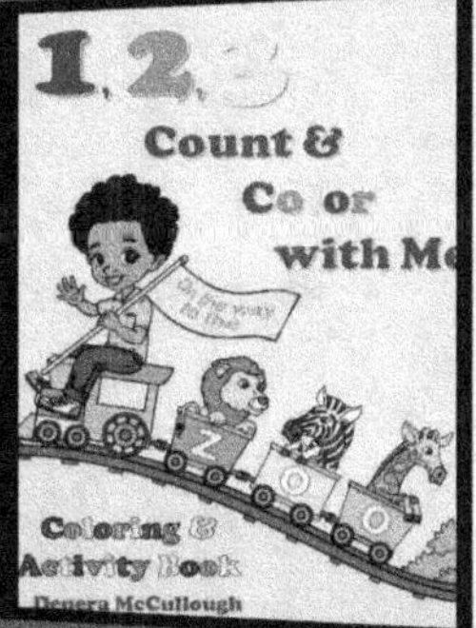

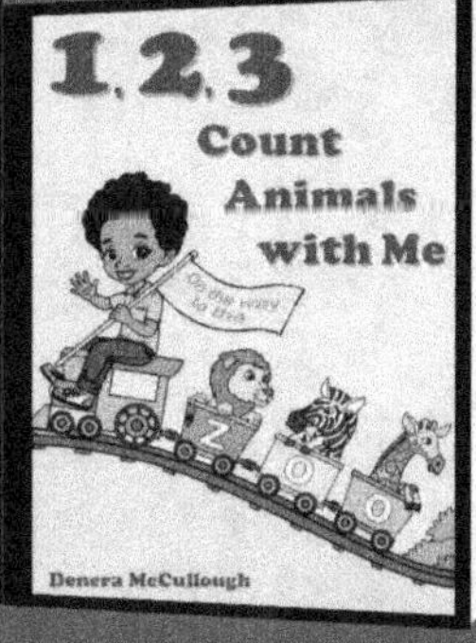

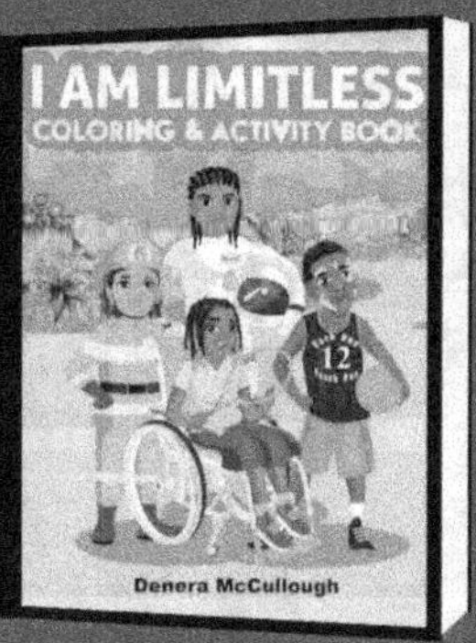

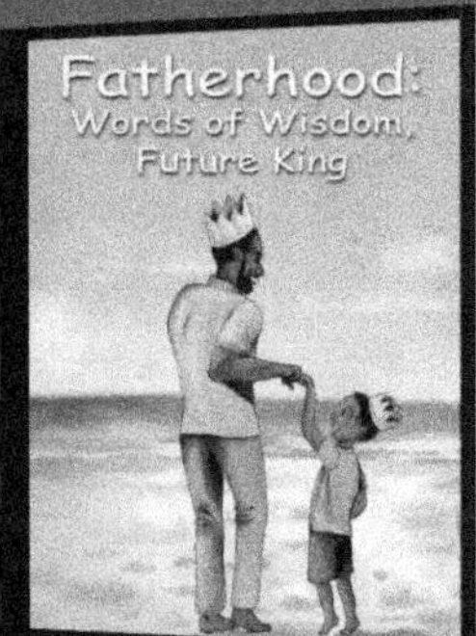

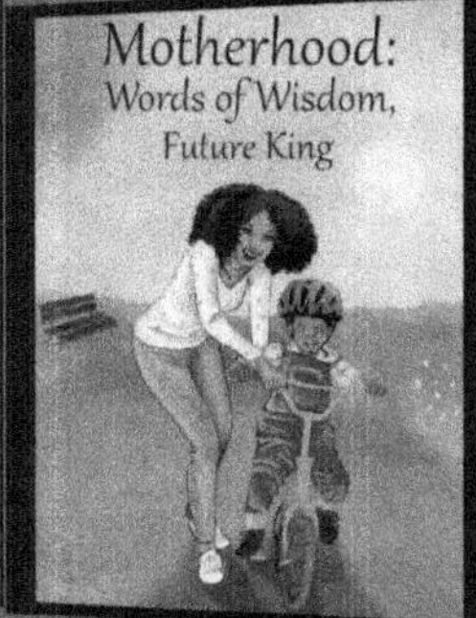

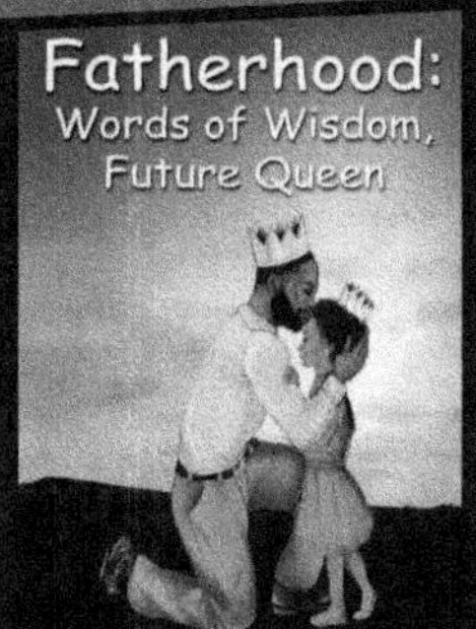

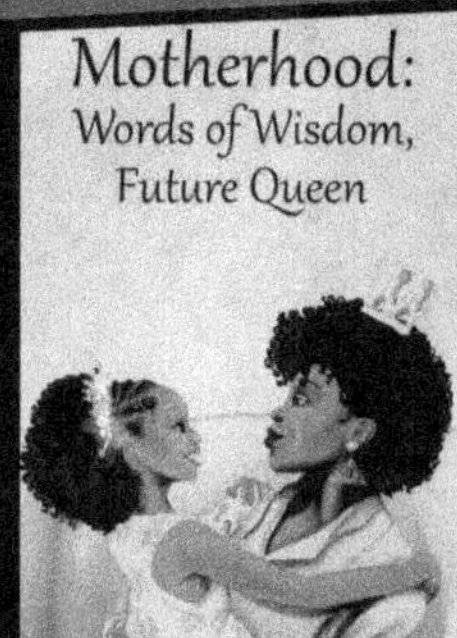

ABOUT THE AUTHOR

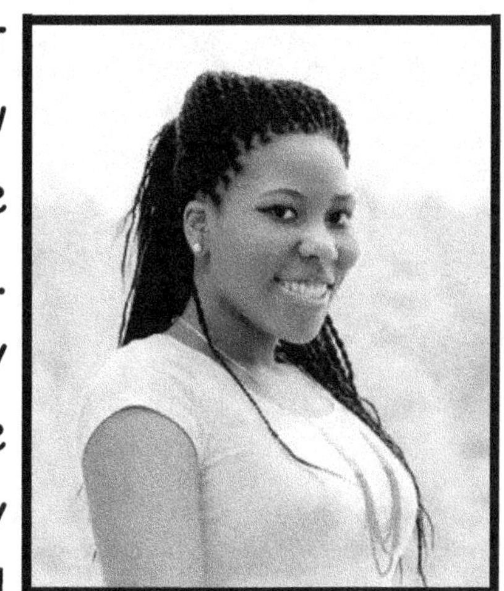

Denera McCullough is a 3x Amazon Best Selling author, who hails from New York City, NY. She is a proud graduate of the HBCU Benedict College in Columbia, SC. Denera values family, education, community service, and self-love. She teaches these values to her toddler through story time, every night. This nightly routine was instrumental in McCullough's realization of the disparity of Black characters in literature, especially in children's books. As a result of her observations, Denera decided to use her family's adventures to create a series of children's books. Her goal is to inspire other authors to write children's books featuring Black characters in leading roles.